THE UNSHACKLED WORKBOOK

A Practical Companion to the Book 'Unshackled'

This workbook helps you apply the principles from Unshackled to your real financial life. Each section expands the ideas in the book with CONSIDER, ACTIONs, and DOABLEs (immediate action steps).

Copyright

Published by Stephen E. Kent stephenekent.com

Printed in the United States of America.

AF722217

Table of Contents

How to Use This Workbook

1. Read the corresponding chapter in Unshackled.
2. Complete the CONSIDER prompts.
3. Perform the ACTION exercise.
4. Complete the DOABLE within 48 hours.

The Unshackled Pledge

My Declaration of Discipline, Wealth, and Legacy

I take full ownership of my financial future.

I live by discipline, budget with wisdom, and spend intentionally

I reject the traps of comparison, debt, and distraction.

I save with purpose and invest with patience.

I build wealth steadily, give generously, and teach the next generation.

I live **Unshackled.**

Signed:

____

Date:

____

Chapter 1: From 'PO' to Paid: A Story of Struggle, Sacrifice, and Financial Freedom

CONSIDER

Think about the first-time money caused stress in your home. What did you see, hear, or feel? How did that moment shape the way you think about money today?

Name one money decision you made from fear, shame, or the pressure to look successful. What did it cost you? What would you do differently now?

What is one money belief you picked up as a child, maybe you never said it aloud, that is still quietly affecting your financial decisions today?

Now that you can see where your money story came from, what does the next chapter of your story look like? What kind of financial life are you building from here?

Who in your life, a child, a sibling, a community, needs you to win this? What changes for them when you break the cycle?

Your turning point happens the moment you decide your financial story is going to change! Your moment can be now. What are you leaving behind, and what are you stepping into?

ACTION

Write one sentence that describes where you are right now financially. Then write one sentence that describes where you are going. That gap between the two sentences is your turning point. Name it.

DOABLE (Complete within 48 hours)

Write it down: In 3–5 sentences, describe one financial mistake or hard lesson from your life. What happened? What did it cost you? What did it teach you?

Share it: Within 48 hours, share that lesson with one person you trust. Teaching it makes it permanent.

Chapter 2: Unshackled Thinking: How Millionaires See the World Differently

CONSIDER

Think about how your parents or grandparents managed money. Name one specific habit, good or bad, that you inherited from them that is still showing up in your life today.

What is one money habit you know is hurting you, but you keep doing it anyway? What does it cost you every month? Every year?

The habit you inherited (Q1) shaped your financial ceiling. Now that you are choosing a different way of thinking, what becomes possible that wasn't possible before?

What is one thing you can do every single day, something small and free, that tells your brain you are a person who builds wealth, not just earns money?

ACTION

Write down one money belief you currently hold that is limiting your growth. (Example: I'll never be good with money. Rich people are greedy.) Next to it, write the belief you are choosing to adopt instead.

DOABLE (Complete within 48 hours)

Pick one limiting money belief from your list. Write it on a piece of paper, cross it out, and write your replacement belief beneath it. Put it somewhere you will see it every day this week.

Chapter 3: Wealth vs. Rich: Know the Difference

CONSIDER

Think about your last three big money decisions. Did you buy what you needed and could pay for, or did you buy just for appearances?

If someone looked at your bank account and your spending history for the last 90 days, what story would they say your money is telling about what you value most?

What would your financial life look like if you stopped spending money to impress others? What would you stop buying? What would you start building?

What would financial freedom allow you to do?

What is one long-term goal that building real wealth, not just looking wealthy, would make possible for you or your family?

ACTION

Write your personal definition of wealth in one sentence. Not money. Wealth. What does it mean to you?

Write that definition somewhere you will see it every morning this week.

Each time you feel the urge to spend money to impress someone or keep up with others, write it down. Just noticing it starts breaking the pattern.

DOABLE (Complete within 48 hours)

Create your three-word wealth mantra, a short phrase that represents who you are becoming financially. (Kent's example: Discipline Creates Freedom.) Write it down. Then this week, before any non-essential purchase, say it aloud. Let it be your filter.

Chapter 4: Buried by Debt: Built by Discipline

CONSIDER

What emotions do you associate with debt?

Think about the purchases that put you deepest in debt. Were you buying a thing, or were you buying a feeling? What feeling were you chasing?

What would life feel like without debt?

What is one thing you are willing to give up, starting this week, to start winning against your debt? Name it specifically.

ACTION

List every debt you owe: the creditor, the balance, the minimum payment, and your target payoff date. Then next to each one, write one word that describes how that debt makes you feel.

That word is your reason to pay it off.

____

____

____

____

DOABLE (Complete within 48 hours)

Make a minimum of one extra payment on your smallest debt this week. Then commit to this: for the next 30 days, no new credit card charges. Track every dollar you spend. Write today's date here as your start date: _________. Today you stepped onto your road to financial freedom.

____

____

____

____

Chapter 5: Winning the War Between Now and Later

CONSIDER

What is the one type of purchase you talk yourself into the fastest? What does buying it feel like in the moment?

Think about one goal that really matters to you. How much closer would you be if you had spent differently in the last six months?

When is waiting the hardest for you? What is happening in your life, your mood, or your surroundings when you spend money you should have saved?

Picture yourself five years from now if you start choosing your future self over your present self. What does that life look like? What does that person have that you don't have right now?

ACTION

Write down every place your money went last month. Then put each expense in one of two columns: Future Self or Present Comfort. Look at the totals. What does this tell you that you didn't already know?

____

____

____

____

DOABLE (Complete within 48 hours)

This week, when you feel the pull to buy something that is not a necessity, stop. Wait 24 hours. Ask yourself: does this help build the life you want, or is it just immediate gratification? Write down what you wanted to buy, what you decided, and why.

____

____

____

____

Chapter 6: Mindset Is the Multiplier

CONSIDER

You earn money. Where does it go? At the end of a typical month, do you have more to show for your income or less than you expected? What is the gap telling you?

What habits sabotage your progress?

Think about the last time a financial setback knocked you off course. What belief did you fall back on? Was it a belief that helped you rebuild, or one that kept you stuck?

If you had to write one sentence that captures your personal standard for money, what would it say? What do you choose to believe, refuse to compromise, and commit to doing differently starting today?

ACTION

Write your personal financial philosophy in three sentences or less. Answer these three questions in it: What kind of person do you choose to be when money is tight? What values will guide every financial decision you make? What standard will you refuse to lower no matter what? That statement is your compass.

____

____

____

____

DOABLE (Complete within 48 hours)

Pick one expense you spend money on every month that you don't truly need. Cut it for the next 30 days. Move that money directly into savings or investing every time you would have spent it. At the end of 30 days, write down how much you redirected. That number is mindset in action.

____

____

____

____

Chapter 7: The Power of Purposeful Giving

CONSIDER

Have you been telling yourself you'll give more once you have more? What has that "someday" cost you and the people you could have helped?

Think about someone who invested money or time in you, or who believed in you when you had little to offer back. Who were they? What did their generosity make possible in your life?

How does giving align with your purpose?

What is the story you tell yourself about why you can't give more right now? Is that story true, or is it a habit of thinking that has followed you from a time when it was true?

If the people whose lives you most want to impact, looked at how you use your money today, what would they see? What do you want them to see?

ACTION

Write down two or three times someone's generosity changed your life. What did they give? How did it help you? Now look at that list. That is what your giving can do for someone else. With that in mind, write the amount or percentage you are committing to give each month starting now.

DOABLE (Complete within 48 hours)

This week, make one intentional gift. It doesn't have to be large. Then set up a recurring monthly gift, even if it starts at $10. Write down who you are giving to and why. Consistency builds the habit. The habit builds the character.

Chapter 8: Budget Like a Millionaire

CONSIDER

Right now, without looking anything up, where do you think most of your money goes each month? When you check the actual numbers, do they match what you expected? What surprised you?

What spending categories surprise you?

What are the three things that matter most to you in life right now? Now look at last month's spending. Did your money go toward those three things? If not, what did it go to instead?

If you found $200 in your budget by cutting something you wouldn't miss, where would you send it first: savings, debt payoff, or investing? Why that one?

ACTION

Build your budget right here.

Write your total monthly income after taxes.

List every fixed expense (rent, utilities, car payment, insurance).

List every variable expense (food, gas, subscriptions, fun).

Subtract both lists from your income. Every dollar left over gets a job: savings, debt payoff, or investing. If the number is negative, something in your variable list must change.

DOABLE (Complete within 48 hours)

Take one automation step: set up one automatic transfer to savings, debt payoff, or investing. Even $25 a week automated beats $100 intended.

Chapter 9: Destroy the Debt Before It Destroys You

CONSIDER

What debt causes the most stress?

What payoff strategy fits you best?

What is one thing you are spending money on right now that your debt-free self would tell you to cut? What would you do with that money instead?

Picture the moment you make your last debt payment. Where are you? What do you do first with the money that used to go to that creditor? Write that picture down. That is what you are fighting for.

When your debt is gone, what becomes possible that feels impossible right now? Name one thing you would do, one thing you would build, and one person whose life would change because you won this fight.

ACTION

Choose your strategy: Snowball or Avalanche. Then plan your first three debt attacks. Write down the account you will target first, the extra amount you will apply each month, and the date you expect to pay it off. That plan is your declaration of war.

DOABLE (Complete within 48 hours)

Within 48 hours, make one extra payment to your target debt. Log it here: Account: _________ Amount paid: _________ Date: _________. That payment is your first shot in the war. Fire it.

Chapter 10: FICO Score: The Silent Wealth Gatekeeper

CONSIDER

What is your current credit score?

What factors influence your score most?

Looking at the factors that affect your score, what is the one thing costing you the most points right now? What is one step you could take this month to start fixing it?

What is something you want in the next two to five years that a strong credit score would make easier or cheaper to get? A home, a car, a business loan? Write it down. That goal is your reason to protect your score.

Payment history is 35% of your score. What would happen to your financial future if you never missed a single payment from this day forward? What needs to be automated or changed to make that a guarantee?

____

____

____

____

ACTION

Pull your credit report from AnnualCreditReport.com. Review all three bureaus. Write down: your score from each bureau, the biggest factor hurting your score right now, and one error or issue you will dispute or address this month. You can't fix what you won't face.

____

____

____

____

DOABLE (Complete within 48 hours)

Within 48 hours, set up automatic payments for at least your minimum due on every account. Then set a calendar reminder to check your credit report every six months. Payment history is 35% of your score. Automating it is the single most effective thing you can do today.

____

____

____

____

Chapter 11: Save Like Your Life Depends On It

CONSIDER

What financial emergencies could savings protect you from?

How much money would make you feel financially secure today?

What is one recurring expense you pay every month that you wouldn't miss if it disappeared? How much is it? What if that exact amount went to your savings instead, starting this month?

How would having a solid emergency fund affect your peace of mind?

ACTION

Calculate your emergency fund target. Write down your monthly living expenses, then multiply by three for your minimum goal and by six for full security. Then open a separate savings account and give it a name that means something to you. Peace Fund. Safety Net. Freedom Account. That name will remind you why you're building it every time you see it.

____

____

____

____

DOABLE (Complete within 48 hours)

Transfer the first contribution toward your emergency fund. Emergencies will inevitably come. Having funds set aside lowers anxiety.

____

____

____

____

Chapter 12: The Power of Compound Interest

CONSIDER

Before reading this chapter, did you think of compound interest as something that worked for you or something that worked against you? What changed?

How would your financial life change if you started investing earlier?

What is one thing you're spending money on today that your future self would want you to redirect toward investing instead?

Pick one financial goal: retirement, a home, college for your kids, or financial freedom. If you invested just $100 a month starting today, how close could you get in 20 years? Run the numbers. Write what you find.

ACTION

Go to a free compound interest calculator online. Enter $100 per month, 8% average return, 30 years. Write down what you see. Then try your real number. What would you have if you started today and never stopped?

DOABLE (Complete within 48 hours)

This week, open or contribute to an investment account, even if it's just $25. Then find one person, a child, a friend, a family member, and show them the compound interest calculator. Enter a number together. Watch their reaction. When you teach it, you own it.

Chapter 13: Invest Early, Often, and Automatically (Investing 101)

CONSIDER

What fears or uncertainties do you have about investing?

Do you have access to a 401(k), Roth IRA, or brokerage account right now? If yes, are you using it? If not, name one account you could open this week?

What is the largest amount you could automatically invest every month without feeling it? $25? $50? $100? Name your number. That number is where you start.

If you invested your number (above) every month for the next 20 years without stopping, what would that make possible for you? Write about the life that money would build.

ACTION

Set up your automatic investment plan right now. Write down: (1) the account you will use, (2) the amount you will invest each month, and (3) the date the transfer will happen. Then set it up. 'Done—today' is better than 'perfect—years later'.

DOABLE (Complete within 48 hours)

Write one sentence about your investing goal. That sentence is your reason to never stop.

Chapter 14: Dollar Cost Averaging: The Strategy That Beats Emotion (Investing 102)

CONSIDER

What emotions tend to influence your financial decisions most?

Think about the last time fear or excitement made you do something with money that you later regretted. What would have happened if the decision had been automatic instead of emotional?

What monthly amount could you invest consistently?

What would happen to your wealth if you kept investing the same amount every month for 20 years, no matter what the news said about the market?

Key takeaway: Dollar Cost Averaging makes market fluctuations work for you. What does that mean for how you will invest going forward?

ACTION

Write down your investment plan: (1) How much will you invest each month? (2) Which account will you use? (3) What date will the transfer happen? Now, set it up. Same amount, same day, every month. That's the whole strategy.

DOABLE (Complete within 48 hours)

Make your first automatic investment this week, even if it's just $25. Then commit to keeping it going for 12 months no matter what the market does. Write that commitment here: I will invest $______ every month for the next 12 months. Sign it. Date it. Celebrate it!

Chapter 15: Time In, Not Timing: Mastering the Long Game (Investing 103)

CONSIDER

What financial decisions have you delayed waiting for the 'perfect moment'?

Pick one long-term financial goal. What would it look like if you made one small move toward it every single month for the next 10 years without stopping? What would exist that doesn't exist today?

What pulls you off course? What headline, hot tip, or temptation has made you second-guess your long-term plan in the past? How did it turn out?

The chapter says: 'Discipline, not drama. Time, not timing.' Write your own one-line rule for how you will invest going forward. Something you can read when the market makes you nervous.

ACTION

Write your 10 to 20 year financial vision. Answer three things: (1) What does your life look like when you've won the long game? (2) What does your net worth need to be to live that life? (3) What is one habit you will never stop doing between now and then?

DOABLE (Complete within 48 hours)

This week, write 'I invest for decades, not headlines' somewhere you'll see it every day. Then take one concrete action toward your long-term vision: make a contribution, set up an automatic transfer, or open an account. Small. Consistent. Starting now.

Chapter 16: From Scarcity to Security: Why I Built Multiple Streams of Income

CONSIDER

What would happen if your primary income disappeared tomorrow?

What skills could you use to create additional income streams?

What side opportunities interest you most?

What is the real reason you haven't started creating multiple incomes yet? Is it time, money, fear of failing, not knowing where to begin? Name the one thing standing between you and your first step.

If you had two or three income streams instead of one, what would you do differently with your life? What decision would you make that you're currently afraid to make?

ACTION

Write down three ways you could earn money outside your main job using skills or interests you already have. Next to each one, write how long it would realistically take to start earning. Circle the one you could begin this month.

DOABLE (Complete within 48 hours)

Take one concrete action toward the income idea you circled. Send one email. Make one call. Sign up for one platform. Research one thing. Write down exactly what you will do and when: Action: _________ Date: _________.

Chapter 17: Armor Up: Protect Your House

CONSIDER

What would hurt your family most financially if it happened tomorrow: job loss, a health crisis, your death, or a lawsuit? Which of those do you have zero protection against right now?

Do you have a will? If you died tonight, would your family know exactly what to do and who gets what? If the answer is no, what is stopping you from fixing that this month?

Most people avoid creating a will or reviewing their insurance because it forces them to confront mortality. What specifically makes you uncomfortable about these conversations? And what does that discomfort cost your family if you never have them?

Think about someone you know — a friend, family member, or coworker — who faced a financial crisis because they were unprotected: no life insurance, no will, no disability coverage. What happened to them? What would you do differently in your own life because of what you saw?

ACTION

Review every insurance policy you have: health, life, home or renters, car. For each one, write down the coverage amount and when you last updated it. Then identify the one policy you need to add or increase right now.

____

____

____

____

Create your Protection Checklist right now. For each item below, write "Have It," "Need It," or "Need to Update It":

Health Insurance: __________ | Disability Insurance: __________ | Term Life Insurance: __________ | Homeowners or Renters Insurance: __________ | Umbrella Policy: __________ | Will: __________ | Power of Attorney: __________ | Healthcare Directive: __________

Every blank marked "Need It" or "Need to Update It" is a gap in your family's armor. Prioritize the top two and set a deadline to address them this month. Write those deadlines here: (1) __________ by __________ (2) __________ by __________

DOABLE (Complete within 48 hours)

Pick the one thing you know you are missing, a life insurance policy, a will, a disability plan, and take one concrete step toward getting it. Look up a quote. Call an agent. Open a document. Write down what you did: Action taken: __________ Date: __________. Now, ensure you take care of your other missing items.

____

____

____

____

Chapter 18: Understanding Taxes: Keep More of What You Make

CONSIDER

What percentage of your check went to taxes before you ever saw it? Did that number surprise you?

Do you have a 401(k), Roth IRA, or Health Savings Account (HSA) right now? If not, do you know how much tax you could save each year by starting one?

Think about your spending last year. What did you spend money on for work, health, or your future that you never got credit for on your taxes? What would you do differently this year?

When did you last sit down with a tax professional, not just file your return, but talk through ways to keep more of what you earn? What would change if you did that before this tax year ends?

ACTION

Write down every tax-friendly account you currently use: 401(k), Roth IRA, HSA, etc. Then write down the one you are NOT using that you could open this month. That one account could save you hundreds or thousands of dollars a year.

DOABLE (Complete within 48 hours)

Look up one account or deduction from this chapter you are not currently using. Write down what it is, how much it could save you, and make one step towards setting it up this week.

Chapter 19: Legacy Building: Moving Beyond Yourself

CONSIDER

When the people you love most talk about you after you're gone, what do you want them to say? Not about your money, but about your identity and values.

____

____

____

____

What values should your wealth represent?

____

____

____

____

What is the one thing you know now about money, discipline, or faith that you wish someone had told you earlier? Who in your life needs to hear it from you?

____

____

____

____

What causes or communities matter most to you?

____

____

____

____

If you started doing one thing differently today that your children or the people you mentor could watch and copy, what would that one thing be?

____

ACTION

Write your legacy statement in one sentence. Start with: 'I want to be remembered for...' Make it specific. Make it true. Let it become the filter for every major decision you make from here forward."

DOABLE (Complete within 48 hours)

Share one financial lesson with someone younger this week. Explain why this is so important.

Chapter 20: Uncomfortable Obedience: You Weren't Created to Play Small

CONSIDER

What dreams have you delayed because they felt intimidating?

Think beyond money for a moment. What is the boldest thing GOD or life is asking you to do right now that you have been putting off? What is the cost of saying no to it?

What purpose-driven goals motivate you most?

You've named the bold move. You've named the fear. Now name the date. What is the one uncomfortable thing you will do this week, not someday, this week? Growth is on the other side of discomfort.

ACTION

Write down the one bold goal that keeps coming back to you no matter how many times you push it away. Then write the first small step toward it. Not the whole plan. Just the first step. And next to it, write why you believe you were meant to pursue this.

____

____

____

____

DOABLE (Complete within 48 hours)

This week, do the uncomfortable thing you named. Not when it feels right. Now. Write down what you will do and when: Bold action: _________ Date: _________. Discomfort is proof you're growing.

____

____

____

____

Chapter 21: The Psychology of Money

CONSIDER

What emotions most influence your financial decisions?

Think of one moment from your past when money caused real pain or real fear in your life. How does that moment still show up in the way you manage money today?

When was the last time you bought something to feel better, not because you needed it? What were you feeling before you bought it?

The next time you feel the urge to spend money for the wrong reasons, what is one question you could ask yourself to stop the cycle? Write that question down.

Which money habit have you stopped? And what habit are you choosing to replace it with, starting today?

____

____

____

____

ACTION

Write your money story in three parts:

(1) Where it started: What did you learn about money growing up?

(2) What changed: What mistakes, hardships, or breakthroughs shaped how you think about money now?

(3) Where you're going: What kind of relationship with money are you choosing from today forward?

____

____

____

____

DOABLE (Complete within 48 hours)

Write one new belief you are choosing instead of an outdated belief you once had.

____

____

____

____

Chapter 22: The Comparison Trap: When Lifestyle Lies to You

CONSIDER

Think about the last time you spent money partly because of something you saw on social media or in someone else's life. What did you buy? What were you really trying to feel?

____

____

____

____

What purchases have you made just to keep up with others?

____

____

____

____

What is one financial goal that matters more to you than looking successful? What does it cost you to keep chasing appearances instead of that goal?

____

____

____

____

What personal values should guide your spending?

____

____

____

____

ACTION

Write your definition of financial freedom in two or three sentences. Then write down one purchase you are choosing NOT to make this month because it doesn't match that definition. Put that money toward something that does.

DOABLE (Complete within 48 hours)

Unfollow or mute one social media account that encourages unhealthy financial comparison.

Chapter 23: Pay Creep: When More Money Still Isn't Enough

CONSIDER

When your income increased in the past, what expenses increased as well?

____

____

____

____

What is the biggest thing you are spending money on now that you were not spending money on two years ago? Was it a deliberate choice or did it just happen?

____

____

____

____

Out of every dollar you earn, how much goes to savings or investing? If you don't know the number, what does that tell you?

____

____

____

____

What is one rule you could make right now about how you manage every future pay-raise? Write it down. For example: 50% goes to savings and investing, 50% to lifestyle. What's your rule?

____

____

____

____

What would happen if your lifestyle remained the same while your income increased?

____

____

____

____

ACTION

Write your raise rule right now. Every time your income goes up, here is exactly where the extra money goes: _____% to savings, __% to investing, ____% to giving, ______% to lifestyle. The percentages must add up to 100. That rule is your protection against pay creep.

____

____

____

____

DOABLE (Complete within 48 hours)

This week, increase your automatic savings or investing transfer by even $25. Don't wait for the next pay-raise. Start the habit now. Write down what you set up: Amount: __________ Account: __________ Start date: __________. Your future self will thank you.

____

____

____

____

Chapter 24: Your Network Is Your Net Worth

CONSIDER

Who are the five people who influence your financial thinking most?

Which relationships encourage financial discipline and growth?

Which relationships unintentionally encourage poor financial habits?

Who is one person, living or not, whose financial wisdom you wish you had direct access to? If you could ask them one question about money, what would it be?

Is there one group, class, mastermind, or community you have been thinking about joining that would push your thinking about money and wealth? What is stopping you from joining it this month?

____

____

____

____

ACTION

Write down three people whose financial thinking you want to learn from. They can be people you know personally or people whose work you follow. Next to each one, write one specific way you could learn from them this month. Then pick one and do it this week.

____

____

____

____

DOABLE (Complete within 48 hours)

Reach out to one person this week to discuss financial growth or mentorship.

____

____

____

____

Chapter 25: Entrepreneurship: Creating Instead of Chasing Opportunities

CONSIDER

What skills or talents could potentially generate additional income?

How could starting or expanding a business in your community address its current challenges?

What is the one thing you keep telling yourself about why you can't start? Write it down. Now ask yourself: is that a fact, or is it a story you've been telling yourself for too long?

What do you do when people stop and say, 'you're really good at that'? What comes so naturally to you that you forget other people struggle with it? Explore that as a business idea.

If you had to do something this week that moved you one inch closer to building something of your own, what would it be? Not a plan. One action. What is it?

____

____

____

____

ACTION

Pick the idea that excites you most. Then answer three questions:

(1) What problem does it solve?

(2) Who needs it?

(3) How could you get paid for it? That's your starting point. It doesn't have to be perfect. Just write it down.

____

____

____

____

DOABLE (Complete within 48 hours)

This week, take one concrete step toward the idea you outlined. Research it, talk to someone who does it, or test it with one person. Write down what you will do: Action: __________ Date: __________. **<u>Start before</u>** you feel ready.

____

____

____

____

Chapter 26: Staying Free: Protecting Your Progress Once You're Unshackled

CONSIDER

What habits have helped you achieve financial progress so far?

What is the one habit or temptation that has the best chance of pulling you back? Not in theory. In your life. Name it.

Who in your life will tell you the truth about your money when you need to hear it? Do they know you want them to hold you to it?

What is one rule about money that you will never break, no matter what? Write it down. Post it where you'll see it. That rule is your guard.

The chapter says **complacency is** not rest. It's **regression**. What does that mean for where you are right now? What would you tell your future self to never stop doing?

ACTION

Write your protection plan. Answer three things:

(1) What is your emergency plan if income stops?

(2) Which core habit will you recommit to this week?

(3) Who is your accountability partner and when will you check in with them next?

DOABLE (Complete within 48 hours)

Share your financial goals with a trusted accountability partner.

Chapter 27: Faith in the Financial Fight

CONSIDER

How has faith influenced your financial journey?

What moments tested your belief in your financial future?

Do you tithe, give, or set aside money as an act of faith? If yes, how has that shaped your view of what you have?

When was the last time you looked back at where you started financially and thanked GOD for how far you've come? What would change if you made that a regular habit?

When financial fear rises, what do you hold onto? A verse, a prayer, a promise, a memory of how GOD came through before? If you don't have an anchor yet, what would you want it to be?

ACTION

Write a prayer over your financial life right now. Three parts: (1) What you are giving to GOD, (2) What you are trusting HIM to provide, (3) What you are committing to build. Keep it. Read it every week.

DOABLE (Complete within 48 hours)

Within 48 hours, write down one financial blessing you have right now and thank GOD for it. Then choose one verse about money, stewardship, or trust, write it somewhere you'll see it daily, and commit to memorizing it this month.

Chapter 28: Mastering Money Conversations in Relationships

CONSIDER

What financial conversations have you avoided in relationships?

What money lessons did you learn growing up, that influence your communication today?

What is one thing you wish you and your partner or family agreed on when it comes to money? What would it take to get there?

Before entering any financial agreement with someone, whether a business partner, spouse, or family member, what are the three most important things you need to know about how they manage money?

Financial trust is developed through consistent honesty over time. What is one honest conversation about money you have been putting off? What would it take to have it this week?

____

____

____

____

ACTION

Write down three financial goals you want to pursue with someone you care about. A partner, a child, a close friend. Then write one honest conversation you need to have to make those goals possible.

____

____

____

____

DOABLE (Complete within 48 hours)

Initiate one honest money conversation with someone important in your life.

____

____

____

____

Chapter 29: From Success to Significance

CONSIDER

Think about what success meant to you five years ago. What does it mean to you now? What changed, and what does that shift tell you about where you're headed?

What impact do you want your financial life to have on others?

What is the hardest thing you've been through financially? Who else is going through that right now? What could your experiences give them?

What part of your story could inspire someone else?

Who is one person in your life right now who needs what you've learned? What is one thing you could do this month to pour into them?

____

____

____

____

ACTION

Write one lesson from your journey that someone else needs to hear. It can be a paragraph or a page. Then write the name of one person you will share it with. That is your significance in action.

____

____

____

____

DOABLE (Complete within 48 hours)

This week, identify one person you can encourage. Send the text. Make the call. Open the door. Write their name here: _________ and write what you will do: _________. Your presence may be the spark they've needed for a long time.

____

____

____

____

Chapter 30: Teach the Next Generation

CONSIDER

What financial lessons did you wish someone had taught you earlier?

Who in your life could benefit from financial guidance today?

If you could teach one money habit to every young person before they got their first paycheck, what would it be? Why that one?

Think about a young person you know. What is one specific conversation about money you could have with them this week that could change how they think about their future?

How important do you think it is to share your financial knowledge with others?

____

____

____

____

ACTION

Write down the three money lessons that cost you the most to learn. Then next to each one, write the name of one young person who needs to hear it. Those lessons are your gifts to someone else.

____

____

____

____

DOABLE (Complete within 48 hours)

Have a 10-minute financial conversation with a young person this week. Be vulnerable. It builds trust.

____

____

____

____

Chapter 31: Conclusion: The Unshackled Life

CONSIDER

What is the most powerful lesson you learned from this journey?

What is the one habit you are committing to, starting today, that your future self will thank you for?

What is the hardest part of the financial life you are building? What will you do when that part gets harder?

What does living 'Unshackled' mean in your personal life?

What legacy do you want your financial life to leave behind?

ACTION

Write your Unshackled Commitment Statement in three sentences or less. What are you "done with" doing? What are you choosing instead? And what will your life look like in five years if you keep that commitment? That statement is your declaration. Sign it and date it.

____

____

____

____

DOABLE (Complete within 48 hours)

Take the one financial action you've been putting off the most. The one that signals you mean it. Write it here: Action: ________ Date: ________. This is how the Unshackled Life begins.

____

____

____

____

UNSHACKLED WORKBOOK SUPPORT MATERIAL

This section provides practical financial tools designed to help you apply the principles from Unshackled to your real life. These worksheets guide you through debt elimination, investing, financial planning, income expansion, and long-term discipline. Work through each tool slowly and honestly. Clarity creates confidence, and confidence creates momentum.

Debt Destruction Plan

Debt can be one of the biggest barriers to financial freedom. The Debt Destruction Plan helps you take control of every debt you owe and create a clear strategy to pay it off.

Step 1: List every debt you currently owe.
Step 2: Record the balance, interest rate, and minimum payment.
Step 3: Choose a payoff strategy.

Two proven strategies exist:
• **Snowball Method** – Pay off the smallest balance first to build motivation and momentum.
• **Avalanche Method** – Pay off the highest interest rate first to minimize total interest paid.

Both methods work. The key is consistency and discipline. Write your plan and attack the list one debt at a time.

Debt | Balance | Interest Rate | Minimum Payment | Strategy | Target Payoff Date

Investment Automation Plan

Consistent investing, rather than sporadic efforts, is essential for accumulating wealth. Most successful investors build wealth by investing consistently over long periods of time. Automation removes emotion from the process and ensures your future is funded before lifestyle spending occurs.

This worksheet helps you create a simple automatic investing plan.

Step 1: Identify the investment account you will use (IRA, Roth IRA, brokerage, etc.).
Step 2: Decide how much money you will invest each month.
Step 3: Determine how often the investment will occur (monthly, bi-weekly, etc.).
Step 4: Choose the type of investment (index fund, ETF, etc.).

The goal is consistency. Even small amounts invested regularly can grow significantly over time.

Account | Amount | Frequency | Investment Type | Start Date

Financial Freedom Number Worksheet

One of the most powerful financial questions you can answer is this: 'How much money do I need to be financially free?'

Your Financial Freedom Number represents the amount of invested assets required to support your lifestyle without relying on active work income.

A commonly used guideline is the 25× Rule.

Step 1: Calculate your monthly living expenses.
Step 2: Multiply that number by 12 to determine annual expenses.
Step 3: Multiply your annual expenses by 25 to estimate your Financial Freedom Number.

This number becomes your long-term financial target.

Monthly Living Expenses:

____

____

Annual Living Expenses (Monthly × 12):

____

Financial Freedom Number (Annual × 25):

____

Net Worth Tracker

Assets	**Amount**
Cash	
Investments	
Retirement Accounts	
Real Estate	
Other Assets	
Total Assets	

Liabilities	**Amount**
Credit Cards	
Loans	
Mortgages	
Other Debt	
Total Liabilities	

Net Worth = Assets – Liabilities

Your net worth is the most honest measure of your financial progress.

Date	**Net Worth**
Today	
1 Year	

Date	**Net Worth**
5 Years	
10 Years	

Income Expansion Map

Many people rely on a single income source for their entire financial life. While a primary career can provide stability, additional income streams can build wealth faster.

This worksheet helps you explore potential ways to expand your income.

Step 1: Identify your current primary income source.
Step 2: Brainstorm potential additional income opportunities based on your skills, interests, or experiences.
Step 3: Choose one opportunity and define the first step required to begin.

You do not need to build many income streams at once. Focus on building one additional stream at a time.

Primary Income Source:

____

____

Potential Additional Income Stream:

____

____

Skills or Resources You Could Use:

____

____

First Action Step:

____

____

Legacy Impact Plan

Real wealth isn't just how much you put aside. It is also measured by the impact you create for others. Financial knowledge passed to the next generation can transform families and communities.

This worksheet helps you intentionally think about the people you want to influence and the knowledge you want to share.

Consider the following questions:
• Who could benefit from the financial lessons you have learned?
• What wisdom do you wish someone had shared with you earlier?
• How can you pass that knowledge forward?

The Unshackled 90-Day Commitment

Financial transformation rarely happens overnight.
It happens through disciplined action repeated over time.
Track your progress each week and watch momentum build.

Lasting change requires consistent action over time. This commitment exercise helps you translate the lessons from Unshackled into concrete goals for the next 90 days.

Choose three financial actions you will commit to during the next three months.
Examples may include eliminating a debt, increasing savings, beginning an investment plan, or launching a new income stream.

Action Commitment #1:

____

Action Commitment #2:

____

Action Commitment #3:

____

Week	Key Financial Action	Completed	Not
Week 1			
Week 2			
Week 3			
Week 4			
Week 5			
Week 6			
Week 7			
Week 8			

Week	Key Financial Action	Completed	Notes
Week 9			
Week 10			
Week 11			
Week 12			

Signature: ______________________________

Date: ______________________________

Certificate of Completion

This certifies that

____

has completed the

UNSHACKLED FINANCIAL TRANSFORMATION WORKBOOK

and has committed to living a life of discipline, wealth building, and legacy.

Signature: ______________________ Date: ______________

To continue your journey, visit ***stephenekent.com***

www.ingramcontent.com/pod-product-compliance
Lightning Source LLC
LaVergne TN
LVHW090332210926
848480LV00004B/1384